# MENTORING

# 101

## WHAT EVERY LEADER NEEDS TO KNOW

## JOHN C. MAXWELL

THOMAS NELSON
Since 1798

NASHVILLE  DALLAS  MEXICO CITY  RIO DE JANEIRO  BEIJING

Published in Nashville, Tennessee, by Thomas Nelson. Thomas Nelson is a registered trademark of Thomas Nelson, Inc.

Published in association with Yates & Yates, www.yates2.com

Thomas Nelson, Inc., titles may be purchased in bulk for educational, business, fund-raising, or sales promotional use. For information, please e-mail SpecialMarkets@ThomasNelson.com.

Portions of this book have been previously published in *Your Road Map for Success, The 21 Irrefutable Laws of Leadership, Developing the Leaders Around You, The 360° Leader,* and *Winning with People* by John C. Maxwell.

**Library of Congress Cataloging-in-Publication Data**

Maxwell, John C., 1947–
    Mentoring 101 : what every leader needs to know / John C. Maxwell.
      p. cm.
    ISBN 978-1-4002-8022-3
    1. Mentoring in business--Handbooks, manuals, etc.  I. Title.
HF5385.M39 2008
658.3'124--dc22

                                 2008026081

*Printed in the United States of America*

08 09 10 11 12 QW 6 5 4 3 2 1

# Contents

# PREFACE

I've been passionate about personal growth for most of my life. In fact, I've created and pursued a plan for growth every year for the last forty years! People say that wisdom comes with age. I don't believe that's true. Sometimes age comes alone. I wouldn't have achieved any of my dreams had I not been dedicated to continual improvement. If you want to grow and become the best person you can be, you've got to be intentional about it.

At the same time, life is busy and complex. Most people run out of day long before their to-do list is done. And trying to get to the bottom line in just about any area of life can be a challenge. Did you know that more new information has been produced in the last thirty years than in the previous five thousand? A single weekday edition of the *New*

*York Times* contains more information than most people in seventeenth-century England were likely to encounter in their lifetimes.

That's why we've developed this series of 101 books. We've cherry-picked the essentials in subjects such as leadership, attitude, relationships, teamwork, and mentoring and put them into a format that you very likely can read in one sitting. Or you can easily toss a 101 book into a briefcase or purse and read here and there as time allows.

In many of my larger books, I go into my subject in great depth. I do that because I believe it is often the best way to add value to people. *Mentoring 101* is different. It is an introduction to a subject, not the "advanced course." But I believe it will help you on your way to significant growth in this area of your life.

I hope you enjoy this book, and I pray that it serves you well as you seek to improve your life and achieve your dreams.

PART I

GETTING READY TO
MENTOR OTHERS

# What Do I Need to Know
# Before I Start?

*If you want to succeed as a mentor, first seek
to understand yourself and others.*

Most people who desire success focus almost entirely on themselves, not others, when they start to make the journey. They usually think in terms of what they can get—in position, power, prestige, money, and perks. But that's not the way to become truly successful. To do that, you have to give to others. As Douglas M. Lawson said, "We exist temporarily through what we take, but we live forever through what we give."

That's why it's so essential to focus on raising others to a higher level. And we can do that with people from every area of our lives—at work and home, in church and the clubhouse. That's evidently what Texas representative Wright Patman did, according to a story told by Senator Paul Simon.

He said that Patman died at age eighty-two while serving in the U.S. House of Representatives. At his funeral, an older woman who lived in his district was heard to have said, "He rose up mighty high, but he brung us all up with him."

## WHY MANY PEOPLE DON'T MENTOR OTHERS

If mentoring others is such a rewarding calling, why doesn't everyone do it? One reason is that it takes work. But there are also many others. Here are a few of the most common ones.

### INSECURITY

Virginia Arcastle commented, "When people are made to feel secure and important and appreciated, it will no longer be necessary for them to whittle down others in order to seem bigger in comparison." That's what insecure people tend to do—make themselves look better at others' expense.

Truly successful people, on the other hand, raise others up. And they don't feel threatened by the thought of having others become more successful and move to a higher level. They are growing and striving for their potential; they aren't worried about having someone replace them. They're nothing like the executive who wrote a memo to the personnel director saying, "Search the organization for an alert, aggressive young man who could step into my shoes—and when you find him, fire him." Raising up others is a successful person's joy.

## Ego

Some people's egos are so huge that they have to be either the bride at the wedding or the corpse at the funeral. They think other people exist only to serve them in some way or another. Adolf Hitler was like that. According to Robert Waite, when Hitler was searching for a chauffeur, he interviewed thirty candidates for the job. He selected the shortest man in the group and kept him as his personal driver for the rest of his life—even though the man required special blocks under the driver's seat so that he could see over the steering wheel.[1] Hitler used others to make himself appear bigger and better than he really was. A person consumed with himself never considers spending time raising others up.

## Inability to Discern People's "Success Seeds"

I believe every person has the seed of success inside. Too many people can't find it in themselves, let alone in others, and as a result, they don't reach their potential. But many do find that seed, and chances are, you are one of those people. The good news is that once you are able to find it in yourself, you're better able to do the same with others. When you do, it benefits both of you because you and the person you help will be able to fulfill the purposes for which each was born.

The ability to find another's seed of success takes commitment, diligence, and a genuine desire to focus on others. You have to look at the person's gifts, temperament, passions, successes, joys, and opportunities. And once you find that seed, you need to fertilize it with encouragement and water it with opportunity. If you do, the person will blossom before your eyes.

## Wrong Concept of Success

True success is knowing your purpose, growing to reach your maximum potential, and sowing seeds to benefit others. The average person doesn't know that. He or she is scrambling to arrive at a destination or acquire more possessions than the next-door neighbors.

Fred Smith said: "Some of us tend to think, *I could have been a success, but I never had the opportunity. I wasn't born into the right family, or I didn't have the money to go to the best school.* But when we measure success by the extent we're using what we've received, it eliminates that frustration." And one of the most vital aspects of how we're using what we received comes in the area of helping others. As Cullen Hightower remarked, "A true measure of your worth includes all the benefits others have gained from your success."

## Lack of Training

The final reason many people don't raise up the people around them is that they don't know how to do it. Mentoring others isn't something most people learn in school. Even if you went to college to become a teacher, you were probably trained to disseminate information to a group, not to come alongside a single person, pour into her life, and raise her to a higher level.

## What You Need to Know as You Start

Raising people to a higher level and helping them be successful involve more than giving them information or skills.

If that were not the case, every new employee would go from trainee to success as soon as he understood how to do his job; every child would be successful whenever she learned something new at school. But success doesn't automatically follow knowledge. The process is complicated because you're working with people. However, understanding some basic concepts about people opens the door to your ability to develop others. For example, remind yourself that

## EVERYONE WANTS TO FEEL WORTHWHILE

Donald Laird said, "Always help people increase their own self-esteem. Develop your skill in making other people feel important. There is hardly a higher compliment you can pay an individual than helping him be useful and to find satisfaction from his usefulness." When a person doesn't feel good about himself, he will never believe he is successful, no matter what he accomplishes. But a person who feels worthwhile is ripe for success.

## EVERYONE NEEDS AND RESPONDS TO ENCOURAGEMENT

One of my favorite quotes comes from industrialist Charles Schwab, who said, "I have yet to find the man, however exalted his station, who did not do better work and put forth greater effort under a spirit of approval than under a spirit of criticism." If you desire to raise another person up, then you need to become one of her staunchest supporters. People can tell when you don't believe in them.

## People are naturally motivated

I've found that people are naturally motivated. If you doubt that, just watch toddlers soon after they learn to walk. They're into everything. They have natural curiosity, and you can't get them to stay still. I believe that innate sense of motivation continues to exist in adults, but for too many people it has been beaten down by lack of support, busyness, stress, bad attitudes, lack of appreciation, scarce resources, poor training, or faulty communication. To get people excited about growing to their potential, you need to remotivate them. Once you help them overcome the old things that knocked them down, they often motivate themselves.

## People buy into the person before buying into their leadership

Many unsuccessful people who try to lead others have the mistaken belief that people will follow them because their cause is good. But that's not the way leadership works. People will follow you only when they believe in you. That principle applies even when you're offering to develop other people and raise them to a higher level.

The more you understand people, the greater your chance of success in mentoring. And if you have highly developed people skills and genuinely care about others, the process will probably come to you naturally.

# 2

# How Do I Adopt a Mentor's Mind-set?

*Mentoring is who you are*
*as much as what you do.*

Whether you have a natural gift for interacting positively with people or you have to really work at it, you are capable of mentoring others and lifting them to a higher level. You can help them develop a road map for success and go on the journey with you as long as you keep growing as a person and a leader.

## Think Like a Mentor

Here are the steps you will need to take in order to become the kind of mentor you are capable of being:

### 1. Make People Development Your Top Priority

If you want to succeed in developing people, you have to make it a top priority. It's always easier to dismiss people than to develop them. If you don't believe it, just ask any employer or divorce attorney. But many people don't realize that while dismissing others is easy, it also has a high price. In business, the costs come from lost productivity, administrative costs of firing and hiring, and low morale. In marriage, the cost is often broken lives.

I learned this lesson when I was in my first pastorate. My desire was to build a large church. I thought I would be a success if I did. And I accomplished that goal. I took that small congregation from 3 people to more than 250, and I did it in a tiny rural community. But I did most things myself—with my wife, Margaret's, help. I didn't develop anyone else. As a result, we had success only in the places I touched; we had complaints in all the places I didn't touch; and many things fell apart after I left.

I learned a lot from that experience, and in my second position, I made it a priority to develop others. Over an eight-year period, I developed thirty-five people, and they built up that church and made it successful. And after I left, the church was just as successful as when I was there because those other leaders were able to carry on without me. If you want to make a difference in the lives of others, do the same. Commit yourself to developing people.

## 2. Limit Who You Take Along

As you begin to develop people, think of it as being similar to a trip in a small private plane. If you try to take too many people along, you'll never get off the ground. Besides, your time is limited.

When I teach leadership seminars, I always teach what's known as the Pareto (80/20) Principle: In a nutshell, it says that if you focus your attention on the top 20 percent in anything you do, you will get an 80 percent return. In the case of developing people, you should spend 80 percent of your time developing only the top 20 percent of the people around you. That would include the most important people in your life, such as your family, and the people who have the most potential. If you try to mentor and develop more people than that, you're going to be spreading yourself too thin.

## 3. Develop Relationships Before Starting Out

The best leaders understand the important role of relationships when it comes to success. For example, Lee Iacocca once asked legendary Green Bay Packers coach Vince Lombardi what it took to make a winning team. Here's how Lombardi answered:

> There are a lot of coaches with good ball clubs who know the fundamentals and have plenty of discipline but still don't win the game. Then you come to the third ingredient: if you're going to play together as a team, you've got to care for one another. You've got to love each other. Each player has to be thinking about the next guy and saying to himself: "If I don't block that man, Paul is going to get his legs broken. I have to do my job well in order that he can do his."
>
> The difference between mediocrity and greatness is the feeling these guys have for each other.[1]

That concept doesn't apply only to football. It also applies to individuals traveling together for a season as mentor and mentee. If the personal relationships aren't there first, people won't travel far together.

As you prepare to develop other people, take time to get to know each other. Ask them to share their story with you—their journey so far. Find out what makes them tick, their strengths and weaknesses, their temperaments. And spend some time with them outside the environment where you typically see them. If you work together, then play sports together. If you know each other from church, meet with them at their workplace. If you go to school together, then spend some time together at home. You can even use this principle with your family. For example, if you spend time with your children outside your everyday environment, you'll learn a lot more about them. It will develop your relationship in ways it hasn't before, and it will help you grow.

Another advantage to building relationships with people before starting on the journey together is that you find out what kind of "traveling companions" you're going to have. As you bring others alongside you for the success journey, pick people you expect to like. Then get to know them to verify your choice. It's the best way to be effective—and enjoy the trip.

## 4. Give Help Unconditionally

When you start developing people, you should never go into it with the idea of getting something out of it. That attitude will almost certainly backfire on you. If you expect to get something in return and you don't, you will become bitter. And if you get back less than you expect, you'll resent the time you spent. No, you have to go into the process expecting nothing but personal satisfaction. Give for the sake of giving—just for the joy of seeing another person learn to fly. When you approach it that way, your attitude will always remain positive. And the times you do get something in return, it's a wonderful win-win situation.

## 5. LET THEM FLY WITH YOU FOR A WHILE

I want to share a secret with you. It guarantees success in mentoring. Are you ready? Here it is: Never work alone. I know that sounds too simple, but it is truly the secret to developing others. Whenever you do anything that you want to pass along to others, take someone with you.

This isn't necessarily a natural practice for many of us. The learning model that's used in America by most people for teaching others was passed down to us from the Greeks. It's a cognitive "classroom" approach, like the one used by Socrates to teach Plato, and Plato to teach Aristotle. The leader stands and speaks, asking questions or lecturing. The follower sits at his feet, listening. His goal is to comprehend the instructor's ideas.

But that's not the only model available for developing others. We also have one used by another ancient culture: the Hebrews. Their method was more like on-the-job training. It was built on relationships and common experience. It's what craftspeople have done for centuries. They take apprentices who work alongside them until they master their craft and are able to pass it along to others. Their model looks something like this:

- *I do it.* First I learn to do the job. I have to understand the why as well as the how, and I try to perfect my craft.
- *I do it—and you watch.* I demonstrate it while you observe, and during the process, I explain what I'm doing and why.
- *You do it—and I watch.* As soon as possible, we exchange roles. I give you permission and authority to take over the job, but I stay with you to offer advice, correction, and encouragement.
- *You do it.* Once you're proficient, I step back and let you work alone. The learner is drawn up to a higher level. And as soon as he is on that higher level, the teacher is free to move on to higher things.

In all the years I've been equipping and developing others, I've never found a better way to do it than this. And for a long time, whenever I got ready to perform one of my duties, I made it a practice to take along the person I wanted to equip for the task. Before we did it, we talked about what was going to happen. And afterward, we'd discuss what we did.

Maybe you've already done this with people. If you haven't, try it, because it really works. Just remember to make including others part of the planning process. You don't want to find yourself going alone, nor do you want to just grab anybody who is available. Your goal is to spend your time with the people you've targeted to develop. And always select people and match them to tasks according to their strengths. Anyone who spends most of her time working in an area of weakness for a prolonged period of time will get frustrated and burned-out. But a person developed in an area of strength will be catapulted toward her potential.

## 6. PUT FUEL IN THEIR TANK

People won't get far without fuel—and that means resources for their continuing personal growth. Any mentor can give that valuable gift to someone he is developing.

Many people don't know where to find good resources or what kinds of materials to select, especially when they're just starting out.

I regularly share books, CDs, and DVDs with the people I'm developing and equipping. And I also enjoy sending them to seminars. My goal is always to "bring something to the table" when I spend time with someone, whether it's an employee, a colleague, or a friend. You can do the same thing for others. There are few greater thrills than putting into others' hands a resource that can help take them to the next level.

## 7. Stay with Them Until They Can Solo Successfully

I've been told that every student pilot looks forward to the first solo flight with anticipation—and a certain amount of fear. But a good flight instructor wouldn't allow a student to take that solo flight until he is ready, nor would he let a student avoid her solo once she is ready. I guess you could say that's the difference between a true mentor and a wannabe. It's kind of like the difference between a flight instructor and a travel agent. The one stays with you, guiding you through the entire process until you're ready to fly.

The other hands you a ticket and says, "I hope you have a good flight."

As you develop people, remember that you are taking them on the journey toward success with you, not sending them. Stay with them until they're ready to fly. And when they are ready, get them on their way.

## 8. CLEAR THE FLIGHT PATH

Even after teaching people to fly, providing them with fuel, and giving them permission to take the controls, some mentors don't take the last step required to make their people successful.

They don't give them an unencumbered flight path. They usually don't intentionally restrict the people they're developing, but it still happens.

Here are several common obstacles created by mentors for potential leaders:

- *Lack of clear direction:* Many times a potential leader gets mentored and learns how to do a job, then he is left adrift, without any direction from his leader.
- *Bureaucracy:* Or she learns how her leader works and thinks, and then she is put into a bureaucratic system

that stifles the innovative spirit that the mentor just engendered.

- *Isolation:* Everyone needs a community of people with whom to share and from whom to draw support. Often if the mentor doesn't provide it, the new leader won't have it.
- *Busywork:* Work with no perceived value demoralizes and demotivates people.
- *Poor or dishonest communication:* An agenda that isn't communicated honestly to the person being developed hinders the relationship and confuses the potential leader.

Once you begin to develop others, check to see that you're not leaving obstacles in their path. Give them clear direction, positive support, and the freedom to fly. What you do can make the difference between their failure and success. And when they succeed, so do you.

## 9. Help Them Repeat the Process

After you've done everything you can to help your people, and they have taken off and are soaring, you may think you're finished. But you're not. There is still one more step you must take to complete the process. You should help them learn to repeat the development process and mentor others. You see, there is no success without a successor.

A great joy in my life has been to see how leaders I've developed and equipped have turned around and repeated the process with others. It must be similar to the joy a great-grandfather feels as he looks at the generations that have been raised up in his family. With each successive generation, the success continues.

This process of reproduction has become a pattern in my life. For example, when I got to San Diego in 1981, I hired an assistant named Barbara Brumagin. I trained her, teaching her everything she needed to know to maximize my time and talents. She stayed with me for eleven years. But before she left me, she equipped Linda Eggers, who is my assistant today.

Perhaps the most remarkable example of development has been Dan Reiland, who was my executive pastor for many years. During the first eight years he worked for me, I spent a great deal of time developing him. Then for the next six years, he took over the responsibility of mentoring and equipping my entire staff. In addition, he has also personally developed well over one hundred people on his own.

Many of those people are continuing the process by producing yet another generation of successful leaders. Dan now develops the staff at 12Stone Church in Georgia.

## LIFT OTHERS HIGHER

The positive effects of developing others are remarkable. But you don't have to be a remarkable or unusually talented person to mentor others. You can raise up people around you and teach them to fly. It does take desire and a commitment to the process, but it is the most rewarding part of success. Raising up others is the greatest joy in the world. You see, once people learn to fly, they're capable of going just about anywhere. And sometimes when they're flying high, they help you along too.

Take others with you and help them change their lives for the better. Nothing in life is more fun—or has a greater return. You'll never regret the time you invest in people.

# PART II

---

# ENGAGING IN THE
# MENTORING PROCESS

## 3

---

# WHOM SHOULD I MENTOR?

*Invest your time in people
who will give the greatest return.*

Over time I've learned this meaningful lesson: The people closest to me determine my level of success or failure. The better they are, the better I am. And if I want to go to the highest level, I can do it only with the help of other people. We have to take each other higher.

I discovered this truth about fifteen years ago as I approached my fortieth birthday. At that time I already felt very successful. I was the leader of the largest church in my denomination. I had published five books. I was recognized as an authority on leadership, and I was teaching the subject live in conferences and via audio lessons every month. I was fulfilling the purpose for which I was created, daily growing to my potential, and sowing seeds that benefited others. But my desire was to make an even greater impact on others. I wanted to go to a whole new level.

My problem was that I had hit a wall. I was running a large organization that required much of my time. I had a family. I was writing books, leadership lessons, and sermons continually. And on top of that, my travel schedule was packed. I couldn't squeeze another thing into my schedule with a shoehorn and a bucket of axle grease. That's when I made the amazing discovery. The only places where my influence and productivity were growing were where I had identified potential leaders and developed them.

My intention in developing leaders had been to help them improve themselves, but I found I was also benefiting. Spending time with them had been like investing money. They had grown, and at the same time I had reaped incredible dividends. That's when I realized that if I was to make it to the next level, I was going to have to extend myself through others. I would find leaders and pour my life into them, doing my best to bring them up to a new level. And as they improved, so would I.

# FINDING THE RIGHT PEOPLE
## FOR THE JOURNEY

Over the years, I've narrowed down what I look for in a potential leader that I want to mentor to only ten things, and I want to share them with you. Here they are in order of importance. The people I want to mentor . . .

## 1. MAKE THINGS HAPPEN

Millionaire philanthropist Andrew Carnegie said, "As I grow older, I pay less attention to what men say. I just watch what they do." I've found that to be sound advice. And as I've watched what people do, I've discovered that the ones I want with me are people who make things happen. These people discover resources in places you thought were barren. They find prospects where you believed there weren't any. They create opportunities where you thought none existed. They take something average and make it exceptional. They never make excuses—they always find a way to make things happen.

About twenty years ago, I saw a piece in a magazine and cut it out because it's a great example of how someone with a lot of potential really knows how to make things happen. It was called "Sel Not Spel." It said that a recently hired salesman wrote his first sales report to the home office after working in his territory the first week. It shocked the sales manager because he suddenly realized that he had hired someone who was illiterate. Here's what the report said: "I went and seen this outfit which ain't never bot nothin from us befour and I sole em a good order. Now I'm movin on to Nu Yourk."

The manager was in a panic. But before he could get hold of the salesman to fire him, he received a second report. It said, "I done been hear fer too days and sole them haff a millyon."

Then the manager was really confused. He couldn't keep an illiterate salesman, but he couldn't fire a salesman who had outsold everyone else on the sales force. So he did what every good middle manager does: he dumped the problem in the lap of the company's president.

The next morning, everyone in the sales department was amazed to see the salesman's two letters on the bulletin board along with the following memo from the president: "We bin spendin weigh two much time tryin to spel in stead of tryin to sel. Lets all try to get our sails up. Reed these too letters from hour best salsman. He's doin a grate job and all you shud go out and do like he done."

Even under the worst of circumstances—or with major disabilities—people with potential make things happen. Dr. George W. Crane observed, "There is no future in any job. The future lies in the person who holds the job." If you want to go far on the success journey, partner with others who know how to make things happen.

## 2. See and Seize Opportunities

Many people are able to recognize an opportunity after it has already passed them by. But seeing opportunities coming, that's a different matter. Opportunities are seldom labeled. That's why you have to learn what they look like and how to seize them.

The best people to mentor don't sit back and wait for opportunities to come to them. They make it their responsibility to go out and find them. It's similar to the two ways you can go about picking up someone you don't know from the airport. One way is to make a sign with the name of the person you're expecting, stand near the baggage claim area, hold up the sign, and wait for the person to find you. If he sees you, great. If he doesn't, you keep waiting. The other way is to find out what the person looks like, position yourself strategically near the right gate, and search for him until you find him. There is a world of difference between the two approaches.

Ellen Metcalf said, "I would like to amend the idea of being in the right place at the right time. There are many people who were in the right place but didn't know it. You have to recognize when the right place and the right time fuse and take advantage of that opportunity. There are plenty of opportunities out there. You can't sit back and wait." Good potential leaders know that, and they don't rely on luck either. According to Walter P. Chrysler, founder of the automotive corporation that bears his name, "The reason so many people never get anywhere in life is because when opportunity knocks, they are out in the backyard looking for four-leaf clovers."

Ask yourself, of the people around you, who always seems able to recognize opportunities and grab hold of them? The people with these qualities are the ones you're probably going to want to spend time with mentoring.

## 3. INFLUENCE OTHERS

Everything rises and falls on leadership. That's true because a person's ability to make things happen in and through others depends entirely on her ability to lead them. Without leadership, there is no teamwork, and people go their own way. If your dream is big and will require the teamwork of a group of people, then any potential leaders you select to go with you on the journey will need to be people of influence. After all, that's what leadership is—influence. And when you think about it, all leaders have two things in common: they're going somewhere, and they're able to persuade others to go with them.

As you look at the people around you, consider the following:

- *Who influences them?* You can tell a lot about who they will influence and how they will go about doing it by knowing who their heroes and mentors are.
- *Who do they influence?* You'll be able to judge their current level of leadership effectiveness by who they influence.
- *Is their influence increasing or decreasing?* You can tell whether a person is a past leader or a potential leader by examining which direction the level of influence is going.

To be a good judge of potential leaders, don't just see the person—see all the people that person influences. The greater the influence, the greater the leadership potential and the ability to get others to work together.

## 4. ADD VALUE

Every person around you has an effect on you and your ability to fulfill your vision. You've probably noticed this before. Some people seem to hinder you, always taking more from you than they give in return. Others add value to you, improving everything you do. When they come alongside you, synergy develops that takes both of you to a new level.

Lots of wonderful people have added value to me through the years. Many of them have made it their main goal in life to help me. They complement my weaknesses and encourage my strengths. Their presence with me on the journey actually expands my vision. Alone, maybe I could have achieved some success. But they have truly made me much better than I could have been without them. And in response, I have always given them my best, trusted them implicitly, given them opportunities to make a difference, and added value to their lives.

There are probably people in your life with whom you experience synergy. You inspire and take each other to higher levels. Can you think of anybody better to take on the success journey? Not only would they help you go far, but they would make the journey of life more fun.

## 5. Attract Other Leaders

As you look for potential leaders to develop, you need to realize that there are really two kinds of leaders: those who attract followers and those who attract other leaders. People who attract and team up only with followers will never be able to do anything beyond what they can personally touch or supervise. For each person they interact with, they're influencing only one person—a follower. But people who attract leaders influence many other people through their interaction. Their team can be incredible, especially if the leaders they recruit also attract other leaders.

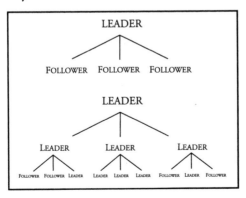

Besides the obvious factor of influence, there are other significant differences between people who attract followers and people who attract leaders. Here are a few:

| LEADERS WHO ATTRACT FOLLOWERS . . . | LEADERS WHO ATTRACT LEADERS . . . |
| --- | --- |
| Need to be needed. | Want to be succeeded. |
| Want recognition. | Want to reproduce themselves. |
| Focus on others' weaknesses. | Focus on others' strengths. |
| Want to hold on to power. | Want to share power. |
| Spend their time with others. | Invest their time in others. |
| Are good leaders. | Are great leaders. |
| Experience some success. | Experience incredible success. |

As you look for people to join you on the journey toward success, look for leaders who attract other leaders. They will be able to multiply your success. But also know this—in the long run, you can only lead people whose leadership ability is less than or equal to your own. To keep attracting better and better leaders, you will have to keep developing your leadership ability. In that way, you and your team will continue growing not only in potential, but also in effectiveness.

## 6. EQUIP OTHERS

It's one thing to attract other people to you and have them join you as you journey toward success. It's another to equip them with a road map for the trip. The best people always give others more than an invitation—they provide the means to get them there.

Think about this as you search for potential leaders: A person with charisma alone can draw others to her, yet she may not be able to persuade them to join her in pursuit of a dream. However, a leader who is an equipper can empower an army of successful people capable of going anywhere and accomplishing almost anything. As Harvey Firestone said, "It is only as we develop others that we permanently succeed."

## 7. PROVIDE INSPIRING IDEAS

Nineteenth-century author-playwright Victor Hugo observed, "There's nothing more powerful than an idea whose time has come." Ideas are the greatest resource a successful person could ever have. And when you surround yourself with creative people, you're never at a loss for inspiring ideas.

If you and the people around you continually generate good ideas, all of you have a better opportunity to reach your potential. According to Art Cornwell, author of *Freeing the Corporate Mind: How to Spur Innovation in Business*, creative thinking is what generates ideas. And the better you understand how to generate ideas, the better off you'll be. He suggests:

- The only truly bad ideas are those that die without giving rise to other ideas.
- If you want good ideas, you need a lot of ideas.
- It doesn't matter if "it ain't broke." It probably still can use fixing.
- Great ideas are nothing more than the restructuring of what you already know.
- When all your ideas are added together, the sum should represent your breakthrough.[1]

You are capable of generating good ideas—probably better able than you think. But you can never have too many ideas. That would be like saying you have too much money or too many resources when you're working on a project. That's why you would do well to get people around you who will continue to inspire you with their ideas. And when you find someone with whom you have natural chemistry, the kind that inspires each of you to greatness, you'll find that you always have more ideas than time to carry them out.

## 8. Possess Uncommonly Positive Attitudes

A good attitude is important to success. It often determines how far you will be able to go. But don't underestimate the importance of a positive attitude in the people around you either. When you travel with others, you can go only as fast as the slowest person and as far as the weakest one can travel. Having people around you with negative attitudes is like running a race with a ball and chain on your ankle. You may be able to run for a while, but you're going to get tired fast, and you certainly won't be able to run as far as you'd like.

## 9. Live Up to Their Commitments

It's been said that commitment is another name for success. And that's really true. Newsman Walter Cronkite declared, "I can't imagine a person becoming a success who doesn't give this game of life everything he's got."

Commitment takes a person to a whole new level when it comes to success. Look at the advantages of commitment as described by motivational speaker Joe Griffith:

You cannot keep a committed person from success. Place stumbling blocks in his way, and he takes them for stepping-stones, and on them he will climb to greatness. Take away his money, and he makes spurs of his poverty to urge him on. The person who succeeds has a program; he fixes his course and adheres to it; he lays his plans and executes them; he goes straight to his goal. He is not pushed this side and that every time a difficulty is thrust in his way. If he can't go over it, he goes through it.[2]

When the people on your team share your level of commitment, success is inevitable. Commitment helps you overcome obstacles and continue moving forward on the success journey no matter how tough the going gets. It is the key to success in every aspect of life: marriage, business, personal development, hobbies, sports—you name it. Commitment can carry you a very long way.

## 10. HAVE LOYALTY

The last quality you should look for in people to join you on your journey is loyalty. Although this alone does not ensure success in another person, a lack of loyalty is sure to ruin your relationship with him or her. Think of it this way:

When you're looking for potential leaders, if someone you're considering lacks loyalty, he is disqualified. Don't even consider trying to develop him, because in the end, he'll hurt you more than help you.

So what does it mean for others to be loyal to you?

- *They love you unconditionally.* They accept you with your strengths and weaknesses intact. They genuinely care for you, not just for what you can do for them. And they are neither trying to make you into someone you're not nor putting you on a pedestal.
- *They represent you well to others.* Loyal people always paint a positive picture of you with others. They may take you to task privately or hold you accountable, but they never criticize you to others.
- *They are able to laugh and cry with you as you travel together.* Loyal people are willing and able to share your joys and sorrows. They make the trip less lonely.
- *They make your dream their dream.* Some people will undoubtedly share the journey with you only briefly. You help one another for a while and then go your separate ways. But a few—a special few—will want to come alongside you and help you for the rest of the

journey. These people make your dream their dream. They will be loyal unto death, and when they combine that loyalty with other talents and abilities, they can be some of your most valuable assets. If you find people like that, take good care of them.

The funny thing about loyalty is that the more successful you are, the more of an issue it becomes.

## Pass It On

I've been very fortunate as I've traveled through life. Not only have I had wonderful people come alongside me and take the journey with me, but I've also had others take me along when I couldn't make it on my own. And that's what life is all about—people helping people and adding value to others.

As you pick people to mentor, focus on people who will not only make the most of what you give and help you. Pick people who will pass it on. Mentoring is meant to be shared.

## 4

---

# HOW CAN I SET THEM UP
# FOR SUCCESS?

*See everyone you mentor as a "10."*

I want to ask you a question: Who is your favorite teacher of all time? Think back through all your years in school, from kindergarten to the last year of your education. Who stands out? Is there a teacher who changed your life? Most of us have one. Mine was actually a Sunday school teacher named Glen Leatherwood. Who was yours?

What made that teacher different? Was it subject knowledge? Was it teaching technique? Though your teacher may have possessed great knowledge and mastered outstanding technique, I'm willing to bet that what separated that teacher from all of the others was his or her belief in you. That teacher probably saw you as a 10. The teacher who browbeats you and tells you how ignorant or undisciplined you are isn't the one who inspires you to learn and grow. It's the one who thinks you're wonderful and tells you so.

Now I'd like you to think about your working life and the leaders you've worked for over the years. As you think about them, ask yourself the following questions:

- *Who gets my best effort?* The leader who believes I'm a 10 or the leader who believes I'm a 2?
- *Who do I enjoy working with?* The leader who believes I'm a 10 or the leader who believes I'm a 2?
- *Who is the easiest for me to approach?* The leader who believes I'm a 10 or the leader who believes I'm a 2?
- *Who wants the best for me?* The leader who believes I'm a 10 or the leader who believes I'm a 2?
- *Who will I learn the most from?* The leader who believes I'm a 10 or the leader who believes I'm a 2?

Mentoring leaders get more out of their people because they think more of their people. They respect and value them, and as a result, their people want to follow them. The positive, uplifting attitude that they bring to leadership creates a positive working environment where everyone on the team has a place and purpose—and where everyone shares in the win.

For some leaders, this is easy and natural, especially if they have positive personalities. I find that people who were greatly encouraged and valued as children often build up others almost instinctively. But it is a skill that can be learned by anyone, and it is a must for anyone who desires to become a successful person.

## How to Treat Others Like a 10

If you want to really shine in this area, apply the following suggestions when working with your people:

### 1. See Them as Who They Can Become

Author Bennett Cerf wrote that J. William Stanton, who served many years as a representative from Ohio in the United States Congress, treasured a letter he received from the Chamber of Commerce in Painesville, Ohio, dated 1949. The letter declined Stanton's offer to bring a new congressman as the featured speaker for a fund-raising dinner. The missive reads: "We feel that this year we really need a big-name speaker who'll be a drawing card so we're hoping to bag the head football coach at John Carroll University. Thanks anyhow for suggesting Representative John F. Kennedy."[1] Do you have any idea who that coach might have been? I certainly don't.

Do you have a potential JFK in your midst? Or a Jack Welch? Or a Mother Teresa? It's easy to recognize great leadership and great talent once people have already blossomed, but how about before they come into their own?

Look for the great potential that is within each person you lead. When you find it, do your best to draw it out. Some leaders are so insecure that when they see a potential all-star, they try to push that person down because they worry that his or her high performance will make them look bad. But successful leaders reach down to lift those people up. They recognize that people with huge potential are going to be successful anyway. The best role they can assume is that of discoverer and encourager. In that way, they add value to them and get to be a positive part of the process of their emergence as leaders.

## 2. Let Them "Borrow" Your Belief in Them

In 1989, Kevin Myers moved from Grand Rapids, Michigan, to Lawrenceville, Georgia, to plant a church.

Kevin was a sharp young leader whose future looked bright, and his sponsoring organization, Kentwood Community Church, was glad to support his efforts.

Kevin did all the right things as he prepared for the first service of Crossroads Community Church. He spent weeks talking to people in the community, he selected a good location, and he got his volunteers ready. When he opened the doors for the first time, his hopes were crushed as only about ninety people showed up—about a third of what he had expected. It was a major disappointment, because Kevin had been on staff at a large, dynamic, growing church, and he had little desire to lead a small congregation. He was determined to persevere, however, figuring that in a year or two, he would get over the hump and build the kind of church that matched his vision.

After three years of struggle and little growth, Kevin was ready to throw in the towel. He made a trip to Michigan to meet with Wayne Schmidt, his former boss at Kentwood and the original sponsor of Kevin's church-planting endeavor. Feeling like a failure, Kevin explained to Wayne that he needed a job, because he was planning to close down the church in Georgia. Wayne's response changed Kevin's life. He said, "Kevin, if you've lost faith, borrow mine."

Uncertain about his future, but grateful to Wayne for his faith in him, Kevin returned to Georgia and didn't give up. Slowly, as Kevin grew in his leadership, so did his congregation. As I write this, Kevin leads 3,400 people every week, putting his congregation in the top 1 percent in the United States.

When the people you lead don't believe in themselves, you can help them believe in themselves, just as Wayne did for Kevin. Think of it as a loan, something you are giving freely, but that will later return with dividends as that person succeeds.

## 3. CATCH THEM DOING SOMETHING RIGHT

If you desire to see everyone as a 10 and help them believe in themselves, you need to encourage them by catching them doing something right. And that is really countercultural. We are trained our whole lives to catch people doing something wrong. If our parents and teachers caught us doing something, you can bet it was something wrong. So we tend to think in those same terms.

When you focus on the negative and catch people doing something wrong, it has no real power to make them any better. When we catch people doing something wrong, they become defensive. They make excuses. They evade. On the other hand, if we catch people doing something right, it gives them positive reinforcement. It helps them tap into their potential. It makes them want to do better.

Make it part of your daily agenda to look for things going right. They don't have to be big things, though of course you want to praise those things as well. It can be almost anything, as long as you are sincere in your praise.

## 4. Believe the Best—Give Others the Benefit of the Doubt

When we examine ourselves, we naturally give ourselves the benefit of the doubt. Why? Because we see ourselves in the light of our intentions. On the other hand, when we look at others, we usually judge them according to their actions. Think about how much more positive our interaction with others would be if we believed the best in them and gave them the benefit of the doubt, just as we do for ourselves.

Many people are reluctant to adopt this attitude because they fear that others will consider them naive or will take advantage of them. The reality is that trustful people are not weaker than distrustful ones; they are actually stronger. As evidence, I offer the following trust fallacies and the facts that refute them, researched by sociology professor Morton Hunt.

*Fallacy:* Trustful people are more gullible.

*Fact:* Trustful people are no more likely to be fooled than mistrustful ones.

*Fallacy:* Trustful people are less perceptive than mistrustful people of what others are really feeling.

*Fact:* People who scored high on trust are actually better than others at reading people.

*Fallacy:* People with a poor opinion of themselves are more trustful than people with a good opinion of themselves.

*Fact:* The opposite is true. People with high self-esteem are more willing to take emotional risks.

*Fallacy:* Stupid people are trustful; smart people are mistrustful.

*Fact:* People with high aptitude or scholastic scores are no more mistrustful or skeptical than people judged to be less intelligent.

*Fallacy:* Trustful people rely on others to direct their lives for them; mistrustful people rely on themselves.

*Fact:* The opposite is true. People who feel controlled

by outside persons and forces are more mistrustful, while those who feel in charge of their lives are more trustful.

*Fallacy:* Trustful people are no more trustworthy than mistrustful people.

*Fact:* Mistrustful people are less trustworthy. Research validates what the ancient Greeks used to say: "He who mistrusts most should be trusted least."[2]

I'm not saying that you should become like an ostrich and stick your head in the sand. All I'm suggesting is that you give others the same consideration you give yourself. It's not a lot to ask, and the dividends it will pay you relationally can be huge.

## 5. REALIZE THAT "10" HAS MANY DEFINITIONS

What does it mean to be a 10? When you started reading this chapter and I suggested that you see everyone as a 10, did a certain image of a 10 come to mind? And did you immediately start comparing the people who work for you to that image and find them coming up short? I wouldn't be surprised if that were the case, because I think most of us have a pretty narrow view of what constitutes a 10.

When it comes to improving in skills, I believe that most people cannot increase their ability beyond about two points on a scale of 1 to 10. So, for example, if you were born a 4 when it comes to math, no matter how hard you work at it, you will probably never become better than a 6. But here's the good news. Everybody is exceptional at something, and a 10 doesn't always look the same.

In their book *Now, Discover Your Strengths* (Free Press, 2001), Marcus Buckingham and Donald O. Clifton identify thirty-four areas of strength that they believe people exhibit—anything from responsibility to woo (the ability to win over others). And the authors assert that everyone has at least one skill they can perform better than the next ten thousand others. That means they believe everyone can be a 10 in some area. You can always focus on that area when encouraging one of your employees.

But let's say you employ someone who does not have any skill that is a 10 or could be developed into a 10. Does that mean you write him off as hopeless? No. You see, there are other non-skill areas where a person can grow into a 10 no matter what his or her starting point is—areas such as attitude, desire, discipline, and perseverance. If you don't see 10 potential anywhere else, look for it there.

## 6. Place People in Their Strength Zones

If it's in your power, help people find their best place in their careers. As you think about the people you mentor, try to do the following for each individual:

- *Discover Their True Strengths.* Most people do not discover their strengths on their own. They often get drawn into the routine of day-to-day living and simply get busy. They rarely explore their strengths or reflect on their successes or failures. That's why it is so valuable for them to have a mentoring leader who is genuinely interested in helping them recognize their strengths.

  There are many helpful tools available that you can use to aid people in the process of self-discovery, but often the most valuable help you can give will be based on your personal observations.

- *Give Them the Right Job.* Moving someone from a job he hates to the right job can be life changing. One executive I interviewed said he moved a person on his staff to four different places in the organization, trying to find the right fit. Because he'd placed her wrong so many times, he was almost ready to give up on her. But he knew she had great potential, and she was right for the organization. Finally, after he found the right job for her, she was a star!

Trying to get the right person in the right job can take a lot of time and energy. Let's face it. Isn't it easier for a leader to just put people where it is most convenient and get on with the work? Once again, this is an area where leaders' desire for action works against them. Fight against your natural tendency to make a decision and move on. Don't be afraid to move people around if they're not shining the way you think they could.

- *Identify the Skills They'll Need, and Provide World-Class Training.* Every job requires a particular set of skills that employees must possess in order to be really successful. Even someone with great personal strengths and a great "fit" will not truly be working in his strength zone if he doesn't have these skills. As a mentoring leader, it is your job to make sure your people acquire what they need to win.

In *The 17 Indisputable Laws of Teamwork*, the Law of the Niche says, "All players have a place where they add the most value." Whatever that niche is determines the best role that person should assume on your team. And it really does make a difference. When leaders really get this, the teams they lead perform at an incredible level. And it reflects positively on those leaders. I don't think it is an exaggeration to say that the success of a leader is determined more by putting people into their strength zones than by anything else.

## 7. Give Them the "10" Treatment

Most leaders treat people according to the number that they place on them. If employees are performing at an average level—let's say as a 5—then the boss gives them the 5 treatment. But I believe people always deserve their leader's best, even when they are not giving their best. I say that because I believe every person has value as a human being and deserves to be treated with respect and dignity. That doesn't mean you reward bad performance. It just means that you treat people well and take the high road with them, even if they don't do the same for you.

It's been my observation that people usually rise to the leader's expectations—if they like the leader. If you have built solid relationships with your employees and they genuinely like and respect you, they will work hard and give their best.

## Always Set People Up for Success

I've learned a lot of things about leadership from many leaders over the years, but the one I still admire most is my father, Melvin Maxwell. In December 2004, I visited my parents in the Orlando area, and while I was there, I was scheduled to participate in a conference call. Because I needed a quiet place to do it, my dad graciously let me use his office.

As I sat at his desk, I noticed a card next to the phone, with the following words written in my father's hand:

#1 Build people up by encouragement.
#2 Give people credit by acknowledgment.
#3 Give people recognition by gratitude.

I knew in a second why it was there. My father had written it to remind him of how he was to treat people as he spoke on the phone with them. And I was instantly reminded that Dad, more than anyone else, taught me to see everyone as a 10.

Begin today to see and lead people as they can be, not as they are, and you will be amazed by how they respond to you. Not only will your relationship with them improve and their productivity increase, but you also will help them rise to their potential and become who they were created to be.

# 5

# How Do I Help Them Do Better Work?

*Equip the people you mentor
for professional success.*

At this point you know how to identify potential leaders, build relationships with them, create an environment in which they'll grow, and encourage them. It is time to look more specifically at how to prepare them for leadership in their work. That preparation process is called equipping.

Remember, all good mentoring relationships begin with a personal relationship. As your people get to know and like you, their desire to follow your direction and learn from you will increase. If they don't like you, they will not want to learn from you, and the equipping process slows down or even stops.

## Equip for Excellence

Once you've gotten to know the person you desire to mentor, it's time to get started on the equipping process. Here's how to proceed:

### Share Your Dream

Sharing your dream helps people to know you and where you're going. There's no act that will better show them your heart and your motivation. Woodrow Wilson once said:

> We grow by dreams. All big individuals are dreamers. They see things in the soft haze of a spring day, or in the red fire on a long winter's evening. Some of us let those great dreams die, but others nourish and protect them; nourish them through bad days until they bring them to the sunshine and light which comes always to those who sincerely hope that their dreams will come true.

I have often wondered, "Does the person make the dream or does the dream make the person?" My conclusion is both are equally true. All good leaders have a dream. All great leaders share their dream with others who can help them make it a reality. As Florence Littauer suggests, you must:

*Dare to dream:* Have the desire to do something bigger than yourself.

*Prepare the dream:* Do your homework; be ready when the opportunity comes.

*Wear the dream:* Do it.

*Share the dream:* Make others a part of the dream, and it will become even greater than you had hoped.

## Ask for Commitment

In his book *The One Minute Manager*, Ken Blanchard says, "There's a difference between interest and commitment. When you are interested in doing something, you do it only when it is convenient. When you are committed to something, you accept no excuses." Don't equip people who are merely interested. Equip the ones who are committed.

Commitment is the one quality above all others that enables a potential leader to become a successful leader. Without commitment, there can be no success. Football coach Lou Holtz recognized the difference between being merely involved and being truly committed. He pointed out, "The kamikaze pilot that was able to fly 50 missions was involved—but never committed."

To determine whether your people are committed, first you must make sure they know what it will cost them to become leaders. That means that you must be sure not to undersell the job—let them know what it's going to take. Only then will they know what they are committing to. If they won't commit, don't go any further in the equipping process. Don't waste your time.

## SET GOALS FOR GROWTH

People need clear objectives set before them if they are to achieve anything of value. Success never comes instantaneously. It comes from taking many small steps. A set of goals becomes a map a potential leader can follow in order to grow. As Shad Helmstetter states in *You Can Excel in Times of Change*, "It is the goal that shapes the plan; it is the plan that sets the action; it is the action that achieves the result; and it is the result that brings the success. And it all begins with the simple word *goal*." We, as equipping leaders, must introduce our people to the practice of setting and achieving goals.

Comic and actress Lily Tomlin once said, "I always wanted to be somebody, but I should have been more specific." Many people today find themselves in the same situation. They have some vague idea of what success is, and they know they want to achieve it. But they haven't worked out any kind of plan to get there. I have found that the greatest achievers in life are people who set goals for themselves and then work hard to reach them. What they *get* by reaching the goals is not nearly as important as what they *become* by reaching them.

When you help your people set goals, use the following guidelines:

*Make the goals appropriate.* Always keep in mind the job you want the people to do and the desired result: the development of your people into effective leaders. Identify goals that will contribute to that larger goal.

*Make the goals attainable.* Nothing will make people want to quit faster than facing unachievable goals. I like the comment made by Ian MacGregor, former AMAX Corporation chairman of the board: "I work on the same principle as people who train horses. You start with low fences, easily achieved goals, and work up. It's important in management never to ask people to try to accomplish goals they can't accept."

*Make the goals measurable.* Your potential leaders will never know when they have achieved their goals if they aren't measurable. When they are measurable, the knowledge that they have been attained will give them a sense of accomplishment. It will also free them to set new goals in place of the old ones.

*Clearly state the goals.* When goals have no clear focus, neither will the actions of the people trying to achieve them.

*Make the goals require a "stretch."* As I mentioned before, goals have to be achievable. On the other hand, when goals don't require a stretch, the people achieving them won't grow. The leader must know his people well enough to identify attainable goals that require a stretch.

*Put the goals in writing.* When people write down their goals, it makes them more accountable for those goals. A study of a Yale University graduating class showed that the small percentage of graduates who had written down their goals accomplished more than all of the other graduates combined. Putting goals in writing works.

It is also important to encourage your potential leaders to review their goals and progress frequently. Ben Franklin set aside time every day to review two questions.

In the morning he asked himself, "What good shall I do today?" In the evening he asked, "What good have I done today?"

## COMMUNICATE THE FUNDAMENTALS

For people to be productive and satisfied professionally, they have to know what their fundamental responsibilities are. It sounds so simple, but Peter Drucker says one of the critical problems in the workplace today is that there is a lack of understanding between the employer and employee as to what the employee is to do. Often employees are made to feel they are vaguely responsible for everything. It paralyzes them. Instead, we need to make clear to them what they *are* and *are not* responsible for. Then they will be able to focus their efforts on what we want, and they will succeed.

Look at how a basketball team works. Each of the five players has a particular job. There is a shooting guard whose job is to score points. The other guard is a point guard. His job is to pass the ball to people who can score. Another player is a power forward who is expected to get rebounds. The small forward's job is to score. The center is supposed to rebound, block shots, and score. Each person on the team knows what his job is, what his unique contribution to the team must be. When each concentrates on his particular responsibilities, the team can win.

One of the best ways to clarify expectations is to provide your people with job descriptions. In the description, identify the four to six primary functions you want the person to perform. Avoid long laundry lists of responsibilities. If the job description can't be summarized, the job is probably too broad. Also try to make clear what authority they have, the working parameters for each function they are to perform, and what the chain of authority is within the organization.

Finally, a leader must communicate to his or her people that their work has value to the organization and to the individual leader. To the employee, this often is the most important fundamental of all.

## PERFORM THE FIVE-STEP PROCESS OF TRAINING PEOPLE

Part of the equipping process includes training people to perform the specific tasks of the jobs they are to do. The approach the leader takes to training will largely determine his people's success or failure. If he takes a dry, academic approach, the potential leaders will remember little of what's taught. If he simply throws the people into the job without any direction, they will likely feel overwhelmed and unsure of what to do.

The best type of training takes advantage of the way people learn. Researchers tell us that we remember 10 percent of what we hear, 50 percent of what we see, 70 percent of what we say, and 90 percent of what we hear, see, say, and do. Knowing that, we have to develop an approach to how we will train. I have found the best training method to be a five-step process:

*Step 1: I model.* The process begins with my doing the tasks while the person being trained watches. When I do this, I try to give the person an opportunity to see me go through the whole process. Too often when leaders train, they begin in the middle of the task and confuse the people they're trying to teach. When people see the task performed correctly and completely, it gives them something to try to duplicate.

*Step 2: I mentor.* During this next step, I continue to perform the task, but this time the person I'm training comes alongside me and assists in the process. I also take time to explain not only the *how* but also the *why* of each step.

*Step 3: I monitor.* We exchange places this time. The trainee performs the task, and I assist and correct. It's especially important during this phase to be positive and encouraging to the trainee. It keeps him trying, and it makes him want to improve rather than give up. Work with him until he develops consistency. Once he's gotten down the process, ask him to explain it to you. It will help him to understand and remember.

*Step 4: I motivate.* I take myself out of the task at this point and let the trainee go. My task is to make sure he knows how to do it without help and to keep encouraging him so he will continue to improve. It is important for me to stay with him until he senses success. It's a great motivator. At this time the trainee may want to make improvements to the process. Encourage him to do it, and at the same time learn from him.

*Step 5: I multiply.* This is my favorite part of the whole process. Once the new leaders do the job well, it becomes their turn to teach others how to do it. As teachers know, the best way to learn something is to teach it. And the beauty of this is it frees me to do other important developmental tasks while others carry on the training.

## GIVE THE "BIG THREE"

All the training in the world will provide limited success if you don't turn your people loose to do the job. I believe that if I get the best people, give them my vision, train them in the basics, and then let go, I will get a high return from them. As General George S. Patton once remarked, "Never tell people how to do things. Tell them what to do and they will surprise you with their ingenuity."

You can't turn people loose without structure, but you also want to give them enough freedom to be creative. The way to do that is to give them the big three: *responsibility*, *authority*, and *accountability*.

For some people, responsibility is the easiest of the three to give. We all want the people around us to be responsible. We know how important it is. As author/editor Michael Korda said, "Success on any major scale requires you to accept responsibility. . . . In the final analysis, the one quality that all successful people have . . . is the ability to take on responsibility."

What is more difficult for some leaders is allowing their people to keep the responsibility after it's been given. Poor managers want to control every detail of their people's work. When that happens, the potential leaders who work for them become frustrated and don't develop. Rather than desiring more responsibility, they become indifferent or avoid responsibility altogether. If you want your people to take responsibility, truly give it to them.

With responsibility must go authority. Progress does not come unless they are given together. Winston Churchill, while addressing the House of Commons during the Second World War, said, "I am your servant. You have the right to dismiss me when you please. What you have no right to do is ask me to bear responsibility without the power of action." When responsibility and authority come together, people become genuinely empowered.

There's an important aspect of authority that needs to be noted. When we first give authority to new leaders, we are actually *giving them permission* to have authority rather than *giving them authority* itself. True authority has to be earned.

Leaders must earn authority with each new group of people. However, I have found that once leaders have gained authority on a particular level, it takes very little time for them to establish that level of authority with another group of people. The higher the level of authority, the more quickly it happens.

Once responsibility and authority have been given to people, they are empowered to make things happen. But we also have to be sure they are making the right things happen. That's where accountability comes into the picture.

True responsibility on the part of new leaders includes a willingness to be held accountable. If we are providing them the right climate, our people will not fear accountability. They will admit mistakes and see them as a part of the learning process.

The leader's part of accountability involves taking the time to review the new leader's work and give honest, constructive criticism. It is crucial that the leader be supportive but honest. It's been said that when Harry Truman was thrust into the presidency upon the death of President Franklin D. Roosevelt, Speaker of the House Sam Rayburn gave him some fatherly advice: "From here on out you're going to have lots of people around you. They'll try to put a wall around you and cut you off from any ideas but theirs. They'll tell you what a great man you are, Harry. But you and I both know you ain't." Rayburn was holding President Truman accountable.

## CHECK ON THEM SYSTEMATICALLY

I believe in touching base with people frequently. I like to give mini-evaluations all the time. Leaders who wait to give feedback only during annual formal evaluations are asking for trouble. People need the encouragement of being told they're doing well on a regular basis. They also need to hear as soon as possible when they are not doing well. It prevents a lot of problems with the organization, and it improves the leader.

How often I check on people is determined by a number of factors:

*The importance of the task.* When something is critical to the success of the organization, I touch base often.

*The demands of the work.* I find that if the work is very demanding, the person performing it needs encouragement more often. He may also need questions answered or need help solving difficult problems. Occasionally, when the job is really tough, I tell the person to take a break—demanding work can lead a person to burnout.

*The newness of the work.* Some leaders have no problem tackling a new task, no matter how different it is from previous work. Others have great difficulty adapting. I check often on the people who are less flexible or creative.

*The newness of the worker.* I want to give new leaders every possible chance to succeed. So I check on newer people more often. That way I can help them anticipate problems and make sure that they have a series of successes. By that they gain confidence.

*The responsibility of the worker.* When I know I can give a person a task and it will always get done, I may not check on that person until the task is complete. With less responsible people, I can't afford to do that.

My approach to checking on people also varies from person to person. For instance, rookies and veterans should be treated differently. But no matter how long people have been with me, there are some things I always do:

*Discuss feelings.* I always give my people an opportunity to tell me how they feel. I also tell them how I'm feeling. It clears the air and makes it possible for us to get down to business.

*Measure progress.* Together, we try to determine their progress. I often ask questions to find out what I need to know. If people are hitting obstacles, I remove the ones I can.

*Give feedback.* This is a critical part of the process. I always give them some kind of evaluation. I'm honest, and I do my homework to make sure I'm accurate. I give constructive criticism. This lets them know how they're doing, corrects problems, encourages improvements, and speeds the work.

*Give encouragement.* Whether the person is doing well or poorly, I always give encouragement. I encourage poor performers to do better. I encourage peak performers. I praise milestones. I try to give hope and encouragement when people are experiencing personal issues. Encouragement keeps people going.

## CONDUCT PERIODIC EQUIPPING MEETINGS

Even after you've completed most of your people's training and are preparing to take them into their next growth phase—development—continue to conduct periodic equipping meetings. It helps your people stay on track, helps them keep growing, and encourages them to begin taking responsibility for equipping themselves.

When I prepare an equipping meeting, I include the following:

*Good news.* I always start on a positive note. I review the good things that are happening in the organization and pay particular attention to their areas of interest and responsibility.

*Vision.* People can get so caught up in their day-to-day responsibilities that they lose sight of the vision that drives the organization. Use the opportunity of an equipping meeting to recast that vision. It will also give them the appropriate context for the training you are about to give.

*Content.* Content will depend on their needs. Try to focus training on areas that will help them in the "A" priority areas, and orient the training on the people, not the lesson.

*Administration.* Cover any organizational items that give the people a sense of security and encourage their leadership.

*Empowerment.* Take time to connect with the people you equip. Encourage them personally. And show them how the equipping session empowers them to perform their jobs better. They will leave the meeting feeling positive and ready to work.

## IMPROVING A LEADER IMPROVES THE ORGANIZATION

The entire equipping process takes a lot of time and attention. But its focus is long-term, not short-term. Rather than creating followers or even adding new leaders, it multiplies leaders. As I explained in the section on the five-step process of equipping, it is not complete until the equipper and the new leader select someone for the new leader to train. It is only then that the equipping process has come full circle. Without a successor, there can be no success.

Leaders who are equipping others have the greatest possibility of success, no matter what type of organization they're in. When a mentoring leader is dedicated to the equipping process, the whole level of performance within the organization rises dramatically. Everyone is better prepared to get the work done. More important, the best-equipped people will be ready for the final growth stage that creates the very best leaders—development. As Fred A. Manske Jr. said, "The greatest leader is willing to train people and develop them to the point that they eventually surpass him or her in knowledge and ability."

# 6

## HOW DO I CREATE THE
## RIGHT ENVIRONMENT?

*Mentoring leaders understand that it takes one
to know one, show one, and grow one.*

Many organizations today fail to tap into their potential. Why? Because the only reward they give their employees is a paycheck. Successful organizations have leaders who do more than just give people a paycheck. They create an environment of encouragement that has the ability to transform people's lives.

Once you have identified potential leaders, you need to begin the work of building them into the leaders they can become. To do this you need a strategy. I use the *BEST* acronym as a reminder of what people need when they get started with my organization. They need me to:

B *elieve in them.*

E *ncourage them.*

S *hare with them.*

T *rust them.*

The *BEST* mentoring leaders are encouragers.

Encouraging benefits everyone. Who wouldn't be more secure and motivated when his leader *believes* in him, *encourages* him, *shares* with him, and *trusts* him? People are more productive when encouraged. Even more important, giving encouragement creates a strong emotional and professional foundation within workers who have leadership potential. Later, using training and development, a leader can be built on that foundation.

The process of building up leaders involves more than just encouragement. It also includes modeling. In fact, the leader's major responsibility in encouraging those around him is modeling leadership, a strong work ethic, responsibility, character, openness, consistency, communication, and a belief in people. As eighteenth-century writer Oliver Goldsmith once said, "People seldom improve when they have no other model but themselves to copy." We leaders must provide ourselves as models to copy.

Mark Twain once joked, "To do right is wonderful. To

teach others to do right is even more wonderful—and much easier." I have a corollary to Twain's idea: "To lead others to do right is wonderful. To do right and then lead them is more wonderful—and harder." Like Twain, I recognize that the self-disciplines of doing right and then teaching others to do right are made difficult by human nature. Everyone can find excuses for not giving to those around them. Great leaders know the difficulties and encourage their people anyway. They know that there are people who will respond positively to what they give, and they focus on those positive results.

## CREATE AN ENVIRONMENT OF GROWTH

Here are the things I have found a mentoring leader must do to encourage the potential leaders around him.

### CHOOSE A LEADERSHIP MODEL FOR YOURSELF

As mentors, you and I are first responsible for finding good models for ourselves. Give careful thought to which leaders you will follow because they will determine your course. I have developed six questions to ask myself before picking a model to follow:

*Does My Model's Life Deserve a Following?* This question relates to quality of character. If the answer is not a clear yes, I have to be very careful. I will become like the people I follow, and I don't want models with flawed character.

*Does My Model's Life Have a Following?* This question looks at credibility. It is possible to be the very first person to discover a leader worth following, but it doesn't happen very often. If the person has no following, he or she may not be worth following.

If my answer to either of the first two questions is no, I don't have to bother with the other four. I need to look for another model.

*What Is the Main Strength That Influences Others to Follow My Model?* What does the model have to offer me? What is his best? Also note that strong leaders have weaknesses as well as strengths. I don't want to inadvertently emulate the weaknesses.

*Does My Model Produce Other Leaders?* The answer to this question will tell me whether the model's leadership priorities match mine in regard to developing new leaders.

*Is My Model's Strength Reproducible in My Life?* If I can't reproduce his strength in my life, his modeling will not benefit me. For instance, if you admire Shaquille O'Neil's ability as a basketball center, but you're only 5 feet, 9 inches tall and weigh 170 pounds, you are not going to be able to reproduce his strengths in the basketball arena. Find appropriate models . . . but strive for improvement. Don't be too quick to say that a strength is not reproducible. Most are. Don't limit your potential.

*If My Model's Strength Is Reproducible in My Life, What Steps Must I Take to Develop and Demonstrate That Strength?* You must develop a plan of action. If you only answer the questions and never implement a plan to develop those strengths in yourself, you are only performing an intellectual exercise.

The models we choose may or may not be accessible to us in a personal way. Some may be national figures, such as a president. Or they may be people from history. They can certainly benefit you, but not the way a personal mentor can.

## BUILD TRUST

I have learned that trust is the single most important factor in building personal and professional relationships. Warren Bennis and Burt Nanus call trust "the glue that binds followers and leaders together." Trust implies accountability, predictability, and reliability. More than anything else, followers want to believe in and trust their leaders. They want to be able to say, "Someday I want to be like him or her." If they don't trust you, they cannot say it. People first must believe in you before they will follow your leadership.

Trust must be built day by day. It calls for consistency. Some of the ways a leader can betray trust include: breaking promises, gossiping, withholding information, and being two-faced. These actions destroy the environment of trust necessary for the growth of potential leaders. And when a leader breaks trust, he must work twice as hard to regain it. As Christian leader Cheryl Biehl once said, "One of the realities of life is that if you can't trust a person at all points, you can't truly trust him or her at any point."

People will not follow a leader they do not trust. It is the leader's responsibility to actively develop that trust in him from the people around him. Trust is built on many things:

T *ime.* Take time to listen and give feedback on performance.

R *espect.* Give the potential leader respect, and he will return it with trust.

U *nconditional Positive Regard.* Show acceptance of the person.

S *ensitivity.* Anticipate the feelings and needs of the potential leader.

T *ouch.* Give encouragement—a handshake, high five, or pat on the back.

Once people trust their leader as a person, they become able to trust his leadership.

## Show Transparency

All leaders make mistakes. That's simply part of life. Successful leaders recognize their errors, learn from them, and work to correct their faults. A study of 105 executives determined many of the characteristics shared by successful executives. One particular trait was identified as the most valuable: they admitted their mistakes and accepted the consequences rather than trying to blame others.

We live among people who try to make someone else responsible for their actions or circumstances. People don't want to reap the consequences of their actions. You can see this attitude everywhere. Television advertisements invite us daily to sue "even if you were at fault in an accident" or "declare bankruptcy" to avoid creditors. A leader who is willing to take responsibility for his actions and be honest and transparent with his people is someone they will admire, respect, and trust. That leader is also someone they can learn from.

## OFFER TIME

People cannot be encouraged from a distance or by infrequent, short spurts of attention. They need you to spend time with them—planned time, not just a few words on the way to a meeting. I make it a priority to stay in touch with the leaders I'm developing in my organization. I plan and perform training sessions for my staff, I schedule one-on-one time for mentoring, and I schedule meetings where team members can share information. Often I'll take a potential leader to lunch. I frequently check with my people to see how their areas of responsibility are progressing and give assistance if needed.

We live in a fast-paced, demanding world, and time is a difficult thing to give. It is a leader's most valuable commodity. Peter Drucker wrote, "Nothing else, perhaps, distinguishes effective executives as much as their tender loving care of time." Time is valuable, but time spent with a potential leader is an investment. When you give of yourself, it benefits you, the organization, and the receiver.

## Believe in People

When you believe in people, you motivate them and release their potential. And people can sense intuitively when a person really believes in them. Anyone can see people as they are. It takes a leader to see what they can become, encourage them to grow in that direction, and believe that they will do it. People always grow toward a leader's expectations, not his criticism and examinations. Examinations merely *gauge* progress. Expectations *promote* progress. You can hire people to work for you, but you must win their hearts by believing in them in order to have them work with you.

## Give Encouragement

Too many leaders expect their people to encourage themselves. But most people require outside encouragement to propel them forward. It is vital to their growth. Physician George Adams found encouragement to be so vital to a person's existence that he called it "oxygen to the soul."

New leaders especially need to be encouraged. When they arrive in a new situation, they encounter many changes and undergo many changes themselves. Encouragement helps them reach their potential; it empowers them by giving them energy to continue when they make mistakes.

Use lots of positive reinforcement with your people. Don't take acceptable work for granted; thank people for it. Praise a person every time you see improvement. And personalize your encouragement any time you can. Remember, what motivates one person may leave another cold or even irritated. Find out what works with each of your people and use it.

UCLA basketball coach John Wooden told players who scored to give a smile, wink, or nod to the player who gave them a good pass. "What if he's not looking?" asked a team member. Wooden replied, "I guarantee he'll look." Everyone values encouragement and looks for it.

## EXHIBIT CONSISTENCY

Consistency is a crucial part of developing potential leaders. When we are consistent, our people learn to trust us. They are able to grow and develop because they know what to expect from us. They can answer the question,

"What would my leader do in this situation?" when they face difficult decisions. They become secure because they know what our response to them will be, regardless of circumstances.

## Hold Hope High

Hope is one of the greatest gifts mentors can give to those around them. Its power should never be underestimated. It takes a great leader to give hope to people when they can't find it within themselves. Winston Churchill recognized the value of hope. He was prime minister of England during some of the darkest hours of World War II. He was once asked by a reporter what his country's greatest weapon had been against Hitler's Nazi regime. Without pausing for a moment he said: "It was what England's greatest weapon has always been—hope."

People will continue working, struggling, and trying if they have hope. Hope lifts morale. It improves self-image. It reenergizes people. It raises their expectations. It is the leader's job to hold hope high, to instill it in the people he leads. Our people will have hope only if we give it to them. And we will have hope to give if we maintain the right attitude. Clare Boothe Luce, in *Europe in the Spring*, quotes

Battle of Verdun hero Marshal Foch as saying, "There are no hopeless situations: there are only men who have grown hopeless about them."

## ADD SIGNIFICANCE

No one wants to spend his time doing work that is unimportant. People want to do work that matters. Workers often say things like, "I want to feel that I've achieved, that I've accomplished, that I've made a difference. I want excellence. I want what I do to be important work. I want to make an impact." People want significance.

It is the job of a mentoring leader to add significance to the lives of the people he leads: One of the ways we can do this is to make them a part of something worthwhile. Too many people simply fall into a comfortable niche in life and stay there rather than pursue goals of significance. Leaders can't afford to do that. Every leader must ask himself, "Do I want survival, success, or significance?" The best leaders desire significance and expend their time and energy in pursuit of their dreams. As former *Washington Post* CEO Katharine Graham said, "To love what you do and feel that it matters—how could anything be more fun?"

One way to add significance to the lives of the people

you lead is to show them the big picture and let them know how they contribute to it. Many people get so caught up in the task of the moment that they cannot see the importance of what they do.

A member of my staff who was once dean of a vocational college told me about a day he was showing around a new employee. As he introduced each person and described each person's position, the receptionist overheard him say that hers was a very important position. The receptionist commented, "I'm not important. The most important thing I do each day is fill out a report."

"Without you," the dean replied, "this school wouldn't exist. Every new student who comes here talks to you first. If they don't like you, they won't like the school. If they don't like the school, they won't attend here, and we would soon run out of students. We would have to close our doors."

"Wow! I never thought of it that way," she replied. The dean immediately saw her appear more confident, and she sat up taller behind her desk as she answered the phone. The leader of her department had never explained to her the significance of her job. He had never explained her value to the organization. By seeing the big picture, she had significance added to her life.

## PROVIDE SECURITY

Norman Cousins said, "People are never more insecure than when they become obsessed with their fears at the expense of their dreams." People who focus on their fears don't grow. They become paralyzed. Leaders are in a position to provide followers with an environment of security in which they can grow and develop. A potential leader who feels secure is more likely to take risks, try to excel, break new ground, and succeed. Mentoring leaders make their followers feel bigger than they are. Soon the followers begin to think, act, and produce bigger than they are. Finally, they become what they think they are.

Henry Ford once said, "One of the great discoveries a man makes, one of his great surprises, is to find he can do what he was afraid he couldn't do." A mentoring leader provides the security a potential leader needs to make that discovery.

## REWARD PRODUCTION

People rise to our level of expectations. They try to give us what we reward. If you want your people to produce, then you must reward production.

Thomas J. Watson Sr., the founder of IBM, was famous for carrying a checkbook as he walked through offices and plants. Whenever he saw somebody doing an exceptional job, he wrote out a check to that person. It may have been for $5, $10, or $25. The amounts were small, but the impact of his action was tremendous. In many cases, people never cashed the checks. They framed them and put them on their walls. They found their reward not in the money, but in the personal recognition of their production. That's what gives significance and leads a person to give his personal best.

We must give positive acknowledgment and encouragement to the producers, and we must be careful not to reward the idle. Take a hard look at your organization. What are you rewarding?

## Establish a Support System

Develop a support system for employees. Nothing hurts morale more than asking people to do something and not giving them resources to accomplish it. I believe every potential leader needs support in five areas:

*Emotional Support.* Provide a "yes, you can" atmosphere. Even when support is lacking in other areas, a person can forge ahead when given emotional support. This support costs the least and yields an incredible return.

*Skills Training.* One of the fastest ways to build people up is to train them. People receiving training perceive that the organization believes in them. And they are more productive because they are more highly skilled.

*Money.* It is difficult for people to give of themselves when their leaders and mentors do not give of themselves. If you pay peanuts, expect to get monkeys. Invest money in people; it always yields the highest return on your investment.

*Equipment.* To do the job right, you need the right tools. Too often a poor leader looks at things from a short-term perspective. Investing in the right equipment will give your people the time to be more productive, and it will keep up their morale.

*Personnel.* If you are in a position to do so, provide the people needed to get the job done. And provide good people. Personnel problems can eat up the time and energy of a potential leader, leaving little time for production.

Create a support system for all the people around you. But increase it for any individual only as he grows and is successful. I have found the familiar 80/20 principle holds especially true here. The top 20 percent of the people in the organization will perform 80 percent of the organization's production. So when structuring your support system, provide the top 20 percent producers with 80 percent of the total support.

## Never Underestimate the Power of a Great Environment

People who live in a supportive and encouraging environment are more likely to succeed. Tom Geddie of Central and Southwest Services, gives a wonderful illustration of what can happen in a such an environment where everyone desires to succeed:

Draw an imaginary line on the floor, and put one person on each side. The purpose is to get one person to convince the other, without force, to cross the line. U.S. players almost never convince one another, says Geddie, but Japanese workers do. They simply say, "If you'll cross the line, so will I." They exchange places, and they both win.

They recognize the importance of cooperation and mutual support. It has been a key to their success in the last fifty years. It can be a key to your success and to that of the leaders you mentor.

# PART III

## TAKING
## PEOPLE HIGHER

# 7

# HOW DO I HELP THEM BECOME BETTER PEOPLE?

*Focus on improving the person,
not just the work he gets done.*

When you equip people, you teach them how to do a job. Development is different. When you develop people, you are helping them improve as individuals. You are helping them acquire personal qualities that will benefit them in many areas of life, not just their jobs. When you help someone to cultivate discipline or a positive attitude, that's development. When you teach someone to manage his time more effectively or improve his people skills, that's development. When you teach leadership, that's development. What I've found is that many leaders don't have a developmental mind-set. They expect their employees to take care of their developmental needs on their own. What they fail to realize, however, is that development always pays higher dividends than equipping because it helps the whole person and lifts him to a higher level.

## DEDICATE YOURSELF TO
## DEVELOPING OTHERS

Personal development of your people is one of the most important things a mentoring leader will ever do. Though development is harder to do than equipping, it is well worth the price. Here's what you need to do as you get started:

### 1. SEE DEVELOPMENT AS A LONG-TERM PROCESS

Equipping is usually a fairly quick and straightforward process. Most people can learn the mechanics of their job very rapidly—in a matter of hours, days, or months, depending on the type of work. But development always takes time. Why? Because it requires change on the part of the person being developed, and you just can't rush that. Like the old saying goes, it takes nine months to produce a baby—no matter how many people you put on the job.

As you approach the development of your people, think of it as an ongoing process, not something you can do once and then be done. When I led Skyline Church in the San Diego area, I made the development of my staff one of my highest priorities. Some of it I did one-on-one.

But I also scheduled a time of teaching for the entire staff every month on topics that would grow them as leaders. It's something I did consistently for a decade.

I recommend that you plan to develop the people who work for you. Make it a consistent, regularly scheduled activity. You can ask your staff to read a book every month or two and discuss it together. You can teach a lesson. You can take them to conferences or seminars. Approach the task with your own unique spin. But know this: you cannot give what you do not have. In order to develop your staff, you must keep growing yourself.

## 2. Discover Each Person's Dreams and Desires

When you equip people, you base what you do on your needs or those of the organization. You teach people what you want them to know so that they can do a job for you. On the other hand, development is based on their needs. You give them what they need in order to become better people. To do that well, you need to know people's dreams and desires.

Walter Lippmann, founder of *The New Republic*, said, "Ignore what a man desires and you ignore the very source of his power." Dreams are the generators of energy with your people. If they have high passion for their dreams, they have high energy. If you know what those dreams are and you develop them in a way that brings those dreams within reach, you not only harness that energy, but you also fuel it.

Unfortunately, some leaders don't like to see others pursuing their dreams because it reminds them of how far they are from living their dreams. As a result, these types of leaders try to talk people out of reaching for their dreams, and they often do it using the same excuses and rationalizations they give themselves.

If you have found yourself resenting the dreams of others and trying to talk them out of pursuing them, then you need to rekindle the fire you have for your own dreams and start pursuing them again. When a leader is learning, growing, and pursuing his own dreams, he is more likely to help others pursue their own.

## 3. LEAD EVERYONE DIFFERENTLY

One of the mistakes rookie leaders often make is that they try to lead everyone the same way. But let's face it.

Everyone doesn't respond to the same kind of leadership. You should try to be consistent with everyone. You should treat everyone with kindness and respect. But don't expect to use the same strategies and methods with everyone.

You have to figure out what leadership buttons to push with each individual person on your team. One person will respond well to being challenged; another will want to be nurtured. One will need the game plan drawn up for him; another will be more passionate if she can create the game plan herself. One will require consistent, frequent follow-up; another will want breathing room. If you desire to be a successful person, you need to take responsibility for conforming your leadership style to what your people need, not expecting them to adapt to you.

## 4. Use Organizational Goals for Individual Development

If you have to build a mechanism that is entirely separate from the actual work that needs to get done in order to develop your people, it's probably going to wear you out and frustrate you. The way to avoid that is to use organizational goals as much as possible for people's individual development. It's really the best way to go.

- When it's bad for the individual and bad for the organization—everyone loses.
- When it's good for the individual but bad for the organization—the organization loses.
- When it's bad for the individual but good for the organization—the individual loses.
- When it's good for the individual and good for the organization—everyone wins.

I know this may seem a little simplistic, but I want you to notice one thing. The only scenario where there are no losses is when something is good for the organization *and* the individual. That's a recipe for long-term success.

The way to create this kind of win is to match up three things:

- *A Goal:* Find a need or function within the organization that would bring value to the organization.
- *A Strength:* Find an individual on your team with a strength that needs developing that will help achieve that organizational goal.
- *An Opportunity:* Provide the time, money, and resources the individual needs to achieve the goal.

The more often you can create alignments like this, the more often you will create wins for everyone—the organization, the individual to be developed, and you.

## 5. Help Them Know Themselves

I always operate on the basic principle that people don't know themselves. A person can't be realistic about his potential until he is realistic about his position. In other words, you have to know where you are before you can figure out how to get someplace else.

Max DePree, chairman emeritus of Herman Miller, Inc. and a member of *Fortune* magazine's National Business Hall of Fame, said that it is the first responsibility of a leader to define reality. I believe it is the first responsibility of a leader who develops others to help them define the reality of who they are. Leaders help them recognize their strengths and weaknesses. That is critical if we want to help others.

## 6. Be Ready to Have a Hard Conversation

There is no development without hard lessons. Almost all growth comes when we have positive responses to negative things. The more difficult the thing is to deal with, the more we need to push in order to grow. The process is often not very pleasant, but you always have to pay a price for growth.

Good leaders are willing to have hard conversations to start the growth process for the people under their care. A friend told me the story of a former U.S. Army officer who was working in a Fortune 500 company. The man was repeatedly passed over when the organization's leaders were seeking and recruiting employees with leadership potential to advance in the organization, and he couldn't understand why. His performance record was good, his attitude was positive, and he possessed experience. So what was the problem?

The former officer possessed some peculiar personal habits that made others uncomfortable around him. When he became stressed, he hummed. When he became especially agitated, he sat on his hands. He wasn't aware that he did these things, and nobody ever pointed out the distracting and unprofessional nature of these peculiar habits. People simply wrote him off as being odd.

Fortunately, the man finally worked for a leader who was willing to have a hard conversation with him. The leader made him aware of the problem, he broke the habit, and today he is a senior leader in that organization.

When you don't want to have a difficult conversation,

you need to ask yourself: *Is it because it will hurt them or hurt me?* If it is because it will hurt you, then you're being selfish. Good leaders get past the discomfort of having difficult conversations for the sake of the people they lead and the organization. The thing you need to remember is that people will work through difficult things if they believe you want to work with them.

## 7. Celebrate the Right Wins

Leaders who develop others always want to help their people get wins under their belts, especially when they are just starting out. But a strategic win always has greatest value. Try to target wins based on where you want people to grow and how you want them to grow. That will give them extra incentive and encouragement to go after the things that will help them improve.

It really does matter how you set up these wins. A good win is one that is not only achieved but also approached in the right way. If someone you're leading goes about an activity all wrong but somehow gets the right results—and you celebrate it—you're setting up that person to fail. Experience alone isn't a good enough teacher—evaluated experience is. As the leader, you need to evaluate what looks like a win to make sure it is actually teaching what your employee needs to learn in order to grow and develop.

## 8. Prepare Them for Leadership

In an organizational context, no development process would be complete without the inclusion of leadership development. The better your people are at leading, the greater potential impact they will have on and for the organization. But that means more than just teaching leadership lessons or asking people to read leadership books. It means taking them through a process that gets them ready to step in and lead.

## Watch Them Fly Higher

If you dedicate yourself to the development of people and commit to it as a long-term process, you will notice a change in your relationships with the people who work with you. They will develop a strong loyalty to you because they know that you have their best interests at heart and you have proven it with your actions. And the longer you develop them, the longer they are likely to stay with you.

Knowing this, don't hold on to your people too tightly. Sometimes the best thing you can do for people is to let them spread their wings and fly. But if you have been diligent in the development process—and helped them to pass on what they've learned—someone else will step up and take their place. When you continually develop people, there is never a shortage of leaders to build the organization and help you carry the load.

8

---

# WHAT SHOULD I DO
# IF THEY PASS ME BY?

*There is no greater accomplishment for mentors
than when people they develop pass them by!*

I was very fortunate early in my career. I've known since I was four years old what I wanted to do in life. And I grew up in a home with a father who was experienced and successful in the profession in which I would follow him. The situation is similar to that of the Manning family in football. Successful NFL quarterbacks Peyton and Eli Manning grew up in the home of Archie Manning, who played for the New Orleans Saints. As a result, they had a jump-start in football that 99 percent of other kids didn't.

In addition to the experiences and exposure I received from just being around my father, I benefited from his strong leadership and mentoring. He was very strategic in my development, identifying and encouraging my strengths early. He sent me to several Dale Carnegie seminars before I graduated from high school, directed my growth through extensive reading, and took me to see and meet some of the great preachers of the era. The advantages I received are too many to list. I am truly grateful for all of them.

The result of my upbringing was that I saw success early in my career. I achieved a lot of firsts in my denomination. I was the youngest person to be elected to a national office. I was the first pastor to change the name of the church to better reach the community. I was the youngest to write his first book. And I had the first church that averaged more than one thousand in attendance every Sunday.

Unfortunately, during those early years, I might have also been the loneliest pastor in my denomination. The good news was that when I failed, plenty of people were glad to commiserate with me. But when I succeeded, few celebrated. I thought my colleagues and I were on the same team, but evidently they didn't see it that way. Many times Margaret and I celebrated alone.

## Good Mentors Learn
### the Celebration Principle

Those early experiences taught us a lot. From them we learned the Celebration Principle: the true test of relationships is not only how loyal we are when friends fail, but how thrilled we are when they succeed. We also learned some things that you may find valuable:

### The Joy of the Accomplishment Is Diminished When No One Celebrates with You

When I went to my denomination's conference following my first year as a pastor, I was excited about the things that were happening in my church. I was helping people, and I thought I was really making a difference in my community. My enthusiasm was unbounded. Much to my surprise, nobody shared my excitement! People seemed to look at me with skepticism or disdain. It really deflated me emotionally. The words of playwright Oscar Wilde were true: "Anybody can sympathize with the sufferings of a friend, but it requires a very fine nature to sympathize with a friend's success."

After Margaret and I talked about it, we decided that we would never let others' lack of enthusiasm hinder our own. And we also became determined to celebrate with friends when they succeeded—and to be even more enthusiastic when they surpassed us!

That's one reason I love doing conferences for young leaders. It gives me a chance to celebrate with them—and to champion their successes. I want them to feel encouraged and keep pursuing their dreams. There's no telling what they might accomplish with the knowledge that others want them to succeed.

## MANY PEOPLE IDENTIFY WITH FAILURE; FEWER PEOPLE IDENTIFY WITH SUCCESS

Several years ago, I wrote a book called *Failing Forward*. As I was preparing to work on it, I lectured on the subject around the country. And what I found is that *everyone* identifies with failure. In fact, when I told people that they needed to learn how to use their mistakes as stepping-stones for success by *failing forward*, the reaction of the audience was audible. They wanted to learn how to fail forward.

What I've discovered over the years of working with people is the following: you may be able to impress people with your successes, but if you want to influence them, share your failures. Everybody has failed, so it's a great way to connect.

The problem is that because people so readily identify with failure, they sometimes have a hard time connecting with success. And if they don't identify with success, they may resent it.

## WHAT HINDERS PEOPLE FROM SUCCESS OFTEN KEEPS THEM FROM CELEBRATING OTHERS' SUCCESS

Frequently the very same qualities that prevent people from achieving success—emotional insecurity, a scarcity mind-set, petty jealousy, etc.—prevent them from celebrating others' successes. They constantly compare themselves to others and find themselves wanting. As a result, they have a hard time getting beyond themselves.

Professional speaker Joe Larson once said, "My friends didn't believe that I could become a successful speaker. So I did something about it. I went out and found me some new friends!" It's sad, but sometimes that's what it takes.

## THE PEOPLE WHO CELEBRATE WITH YOU
## BECOME LIFELONG FRIENDS

Back during the first years of my career, two people outside my family who celebrated with us when we succeeded were Dave and Mary Vaughn. Dave was a few years ahead of me in his career, and he was always ready to cheer me on when I achieved a goal or passed a milestone. Even when my church grew to be larger than his and I gained more notoriety, he never held back. And thirty-five years later, he and Mary still celebrate with us!

## BEWARE OF THE GREEN-EYED MONSTER

In October 2003 at *Catalyst,* a conference for young leaders put on by Maximum Impact, Andy Stanley spoke. Andy is an effective and authentic communicator. He leads Northpoint Community Church, one of the top churches in the country with an attendance of more than fifteen thousand people every weekend. (Just in case you are unfamiliar with the church world, that puts Northpoint's attendance in the top 1 percent of all churches in America.)

Andy's second session was about four negative characteristics that can trip up a leader: guilt, anger, greed, and jealousy. Andy confessed that he sometimes experiences moments of professional jealousy when hearing other successful people speak. He said, "I have to make an extra effort to celebrate the success of other people who do what I do."

That potential for jealousy extends even to Andy's closest friends, including Louie Giglio, who directs Choice Resources. Andy explained,

> Louie and I have been friends since the sixth grade . . . We met at youth camp under a bunk bed while seniors battled it out above our heads. Louie is just a phenomenal communicator. When I announce at our church that Louie Giglio is going to be speaking next week, they all start clapping and we have high attendance Sunday. And then for four or five days the rest of the week everyone's going, "Oh, Louie, Louie, Louie."

Andy went on to tell how Louie always teaches to capacity crowds at his events and delivers outstanding material. And every time Andy hears him speak, tiny pangs of jealousy threaten to rear their ugly heads.

Such feelings could destroy Andy and Louie's relationship, and that relationship is deep. Not only do they sometimes work together, but their families are close, and they even go on vacations together. How does Andy handle the envy he feels? By celebrating Louie's accomplishments. When Louie delivers a great message, Andy goes out of his way to praise him and celebrate with him. And Louie does the same with him. Andy said, "It's not enough to think it. I have to say it because that's how I cleanse my heart. Celebration is how you defeat jealousy."

## Become a Party Starter

Andy isn't alone. If most people were honest, they would admit to feelings of jealousy or envy when they witness others' success—even when the people succeeding are close friends or individuals they've mentored. I know I've fought feelings of jealousy. Haven't you? So how do you learn to celebrate with others instead of ignoring or undermining them? Start by doing these four things:

### 1. Realize It's Not a Competition

It's impossible to do anything of real significance on

your own. It's very difficult to achieve success without help. And even if you do become successful, you won't enjoy it without friends. Life is better in a community of people you love and who also love you.

When I reflect on the value of community, many thoughts come to mind:

*My success can be achieved only with others.*
*My lessons can be learned only from others.*
*My weaknesses can be strengthened only by others.*
*My servanthood can be tested only under others' leadership.*
*My influence can be compounded only through others.*
*My leadership can be focused only on others.*
*My best can be given only to others.*
*My legacy can be left only for others.*
*So I should commit myself to and celebrate* with *others!*

Other people have an impact on every aspect of life. Most of the time, I choose with my attitude whether that impact is positive or negative.

Entertainer Bette Midler said, "The worst part of success is trying to find someone who is happy for you." Don't look at your friends, family, and teammates as competition. Be the rare kind of person who is happy when others succeed.

## 2. Celebrate When Others See Success

Not everyone views success the way you do. When it comes to the Celebration Principle, you must be willing to look at things from other people's point of view. What are their dreams? What goals have they set? What battles are they fighting? When they achieve something that is important to *them,* then celebrate! And be especially careful when a friend accomplishes something that you've already achieved and perhaps find to be old hat. Be sure to celebrate with enthusiasm. Never steal another person's thunder.

## 3. Celebrate Successes Others Don't Yet See

Sometimes people make great strides and aren't even aware of it. Have you ever started to diet or exercise and after a while felt that you were struggling, only to have a friend tell you how good you look? Or haven't you worked on a project and felt discouraged by your progress, but had someone else marvel at what you accomplished? It is inspiring and makes you want to work that much harder. If you *haven't* had a friend do that for you, then you may need some new friends—people who practice the Celebration Principle. And you should definitely celebrate the successes of the people you mentor that may be unseen by others.

## 4. CELEBRATE MOST WITH THOSE CLOSEST TO YOU

The closer people are to you and the more important the relationship, the more you ought to celebrate. Celebrate early and often with those closest to you—especially with your spouse and children if you have a family. It's usually easy to celebrate victories on the job or in a hobby or sport. But the greatest victories in life are the ones that occur at home.

My friend Dan Reiland says, "A genuine friend encourages and challenges us to live out our best thoughts, honor our purest motives, and achieve our most significant dreams." That's what we need to do with the important people in our lives.

I have a confession to make. I haven't always been a practicer of the Celebration Principle at work. I've always done fairly well celebrating at home, but in the early years of my career, I was very competitive. I was driven to achieve, and I was very aware of where I was ranked in comparison to my colleagues. I took secret joy in watching my progress as I rose in those ranks. But as I progressed toward the top, something happened. The achievement of my goals wasn't as rewarding as I expected it to be. I felt that something was missing.

In the late 1980s and early 1990s I finally began to change. When I turned forty, I realized that to accomplish my goals, I would need the help of others. I began to more aggressively develop my employees to lead. At first, my motives were somewhat selfish. But as I helped others to succeed, I found that it brought me great joy, regardless of whether it benefited me personally.

What I discovered is that the journey is a lot more fun if you take somebody with you. It's hard to have that perspective if your own success is the only thing you celebrate. If you want others to succeed alongside you, then you must encourage them, mentor them, and celebrate their successes. Not only does it give them the incentive to keep striving for their dreams, but it also helps them enjoy the journey along the way. As I began reaching out and celebrating others' successes, I found that the success of others brought me more joy than my success.

Now I try to celebrate with as many people as I can—not just my family, friends, and closest colleagues, but also the people farther outside my circle. The more people I can encourage and help to succeed, the better I like it. If you help enough people, the party never stops.

# Notes

*Chapter 1*

1. Robert G. C. Waite, *The Psychopathic God: Adolph Hitler* (New York: Basic Books, 1977), 244–45.

*Chapter 2*

1. Lee Iacocca and William Novak, *Iacocca* (New York: Bantam, 1986).

*Chapter 3*

1. Quoted in Ted J. Rakstis, "Creativity at Work," *Kiwanis Magazine*.

2. Joe Griffith, *Speaker's Library of Business* (Englewood Cliffs: Prentice-Hall, 1990), 55.

*Chapter 4*

1. Bennet Cerf, *The Sound of Laughter* (Garden City, NY: Doubleday and Company, 1970), 54.

2. Morton Hunt, "Are You Mistrustful?" *Parade*, 6 March 1988.

*Chapter 6*

1. David A. Seamands, *Healing Grace* (Wheaton, Illinois: Victor Books, 1988).

2. *Success Unlimited* (magazine no longer in print).

# ABOUT THE AUTHOR

John C. Maxwell is an internationally recognized leadership expert, speaker, and author who has sold over 16 million books. His organizations have trained more than 2 million leaders worldwide. Dr. Maxwell is the founder of EQUIP and INJOY Stewardship Services. Every year he speaks to Fortune 500 companies, international government leaders, and audiences as diverse as the United States Military Academy at West Point, the National Football League, and ambassadors at the United Nations. A *New York Times*, *Wall Street Journal*, and *Business Week* best-selling author, Maxwell was named the World's Top Leadership Guru by Leadershipgurus.net. He was also one of only 25 authors and artists named to Amazon.com's 10th Anniversary Hall of Fame. Three of his books, *The 21 Irrefutable Laws of Leadership*, *Developing the Leader Within You*, and *The 21 Indispensable Qualities of a Leader* have each sold over a million copies.

# BOOKS BY DR. JOHN C. MAXWELL
## CAN TEACH YOU HOW TO BE A REAL SUCCESS

## RELATIONSHIPS

*Encouragement Changes Everything*
*25 Ways to Win With People*
*Winning With People*
*Relationships 101*
*The Treasure of a Friend*
*The Power of Partnership in the Church*
*Becoming a Person of Influence*
*Be A People Person*
*The Power of Influence*
*Ethics 101*

## ATTITUDE

*Success 101*
*The Difference Maker*
*The Journey From Success to Significance*
*Attitude 101*
*Failing Forward*
*Your Bridge to a Better Future*
*Living at the Next Level*
*The Winning Attitude*
*Be All You Can Be*
*The Power of Thinking Big*
*Think on These Things*
*The Power of Attitude*
*Thinking for a Change*

## EQUIPPING

*The Choice Is Yours*
*Mentoring 101*
*Talent is Never Enough*
*Equipping 101*
*Developing the Leaders Around You*
*The 17 Essential Qualities of a Team Player*
*Success One Day at a Time*
*The 17 Indisputable Laws of Teamwork*
*Your Road Map for Success*
*Today Matters*
*Partners in Prayer*

## LEADERSHIP

*Leadership Promises For Your Work Week*
*Leadership Gold*
*Go for Gold*
*The 21 Most Powerful Minutes
in a Leader's Day*
Revised & Updated 10th Anniversary
Edition of *The 21 Irrefutable
Laws of Leadership*
*The 360 Degree Leader*
*Leadership Promises for Every Day*
*Leadership 101*
*The Right to Lead*
*The 21 Indispensable Qualities of a Leader*
*Developing the Leader Within You*
*The Power of Leadership*

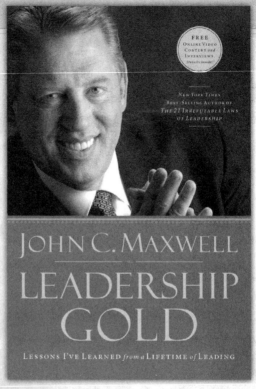